# INNER CHILD HEALING

## Workbook

**Cher Hampton**

# Table of Contents


BONUS: Your Free Gift ... 5

Introduction ... 8

**Stage 1: Reach Out to Your Inner Child** ... 10

Start the Conversation ... 11

Exercise 1: Take a Trip Down Memory Lane ... 12

Exercise 2: Meditation to Empathize With Your Younger Self ... 13

Exercise 3: Meditation to Recognize Your Inner Child's Needs ... 15

Reflection Notes ... 17

**Stage 2: Identify Past Childhood Wounds** ... 18

Do the Inner Child Work ... 19

Exercise 4: Wounded Inner Child Checklist ... 19

Exercise 5: Check Your Defenses ... 23

Exercise 6: Meditation to Heal Defensiveness ... 25

Exercise 7: Identify Emotional Triggers ... 27

Exercise 8: Revisiting Painful Memories ... 29

Reflection Notes ... 31

**Stage 3: Practice Radical Acceptance** ... 32

Accept What You Cannot Change ... 33

Exercise 9: Meditation to Affirm Your Inner Child ... 34

Exercise 10: Fact-Check Your Beliefs ... 36

Exercise 11: Tap Into Logical Mind ... 38

Exercise 12: Embrace Reality ... 41

Reflection Notes ... 43

**Stage 4: Reparent Yourself** ... 44

Be the Parent You Never Had ... 45

Exercise 13: What Parent Do You Want to Be? ... 46

Exercise 14: Make a Promise ... 48

Exercise 15: What Do You Need Right Now? ... 49

Exercise 16: Meditation to Explore Your Own Love Languages ... 50

Exercise 17: Fill the Gaps ... 17

Reflection Notes ... 54

**Stage 5: Create New Norms**     55

  Rebuild Your Life     56

    Exercise 18: Gratitude Letter to Yourself     57

    Exercise 19: Come Out of Your Comfort Zone     58

    Exercise 20: Create a Movie of Your Life     62

    Exercise 21: Celebrate Daily Wins     63

    Exercise 22: Increase Spiritual Awareness     64

    Exercise 23: Personal Growth Quiz     67

  Reflection Notes     71

**Affirmations**     72

Conclusion     76

Thank You     82

References     83

# BONUS: Your Free Gift

I'm only offering this bonus for FREE to my readers. This is a way of saying thank you for your purchase. In this gift, you will find a guide with extra tools to start your inner journey.

***Healing Your Inner Child First Guide***

*Embark on a Transformative Inner Journey to Rediscover Your Inner Child with Extraordinary Tools!*

***Inside this book, you'll discover:***
- How to use journaling in the healing process.
- Questions to remember your Inner Child.
- Space to write your thoughts down.
- Questions to better understand your Inner Child's pain.
- Motivational things to say to your Inner Child.
- Positive affirmations + 5-step method to make your own.
- An extra Inner Child meditation.
- A checklist.
- And more...

# INTRODUCTION

The thing about trauma is that unless it is confronted and safely released, it makes your mind and body a permanent home. However, bringing up the past and addressing the emotional wounds that are still very raw and real inside of you is not an easy process.

The reality is you didn't have a choice of the kind of family you would grow up in, the parents who would raise you, or the various childhood experiences you would be confronted with. But regardless of your inability to choose, the responsibility to rebuild a sense of safety, heal from past hurts, and learn new patterns of relating with people, rests with you.

In the book, Healing Your Inner Child First, you were taken through the journey of understanding trauma, its impact, and the process of breaking free from negative, unconscious childhood patterns.

The purpose of this complementary workbook is to assist you on this remarkable healing journey by offering 23 useful exercises, meditations, and journal prompts. The workbook is broken down into five chapters, which represent the five stages of inner child healing:

Stage 1: Reach Out to Your Inner Child

Stage 2: Identify Past Childhood Wounds

Stage 3: Practice Radical Acceptance

Stage 4: Reparent Yourself

Stage 5: Create New Norms

You don't need to have any prior exposure to psychotherapy to complete this workbook. All that is required is the openness to reconnect to long-forgotten aspects of who you are.

Let us begin the five stages of inner child healing!

# STAGE 1
## Reach Out to your Inner Child

# Start the Conversation

One of the ways to reconnect with your past is to start a conversation with your inner child. See this as the older version of you reaching out to a younger version of you.

Essentially, you are engaging in a dialogue with that little girl or boy, who witnessed traumatic events that no child should ever see, matured ahead of their time due to assuming responsibility early on, and had so many questions about life but not enough answers.

The experiences of that little girl or boy are still stored in your subconscious mind. They continue to make their presence felt through emotional triggers, nightmares, and repeating self-destructive patterns.

Communicating with your inner child opens the door to healing. You get the opportunity to access your subconscious mind through mind therapies and techniques and reflect and make sense of past events, so you can change the narrative and give yourself closure.

The following exercises will help you start the conversation with your inner child.

## *Exercise 1: Take a Trip Down Memory Lane*

Find three to five photos of when you were a child. If possible, select photos that were taken a few years apart. Lay the photos out in front of you and create a timeline. Pick up the photo showing the youngest version of you. As you look at the photo, reflect on the following questions:

1. How old were you in that photo?

2. Where were you? What was happening?

3. Who was present in your life at that moment?

4. How did you feel about each person that was present?

5. Are you sad or happy in the photo?

6. What thoughts were going through your mind at the time?

7. Were there any strong emotions you were disguising?

8. What emotional needs were you lacking at that time?

9. Were there any secrets you were keeping?

10. How does the memory of this photo show up in your life today?

Continue the exercise by picking up the next photo on your timeline, until you have spent time reflecting on every photo. You are also welcome to turn these questions into journal prompts and document your responses.

### *Exercise 2: Mediation to Empathize With Your Younger Self*

Find a quiet room where you can sit alone for 10–15 minutes and practice the following guided meditation. Bring a pen and notebook with you to take down notes during or after the meditation.

Record yourself narrating the instructions below, then play the recording back to yourself.

Instructions for meditation:

1. Sit in a comfortable position on a chair.

2. Take a deep breath and when you exhale, allow the weight of your body to sink into the chair. Relax your face, neck, shoulders, and back.

3. Close your eyes and take deep breaths. Inhale for three counts, hold your breath for another three counts, then slowly exhale for three counts. Repeat this breathing pattern two more times.

4. With your eyes still closed, recall a past childhood memory. It can be a positive or negative memory.

5. Relive the memory as though you had possessed your younger self's body. See what is taking place from their eyes and feel the physical sensations going through their body.

6. Avoid making an adult interpretation of what is happening. Instead, accept their worldview and perception of reality as being true.

7. In your notebook, write down thoughts, emotions, and physical sensations that come up for you. To avoid breaking from your meditative state, stick to keywords or short phrases. Once again, you are writing down what your younger self thinks and feels about what's taking place, not how your adult self interprets it.

8. Replay the memory a number of times, until you feel that you have understood your younger self's perspective.

9. Take three deep breaths and open your eyes. Look at your notes and reflect on what you wrote down.

## *Exercise 3: Mediation to Recognize Your Inner Child's Needs*

Below is another meditation to connect with your inner child. Bring a pen and notebook into this session too.

Record yourself narrating the instructions below, then play the recording back to yourself.

Instructions for meditation:

1. Sit in a comfortable position on a chair.
2. Take a deep breath and when you exhale, allow the weight of your body to sink into the chair. Relax your face, neck, shoulders, and back.
3. Close your eyes and take deep breaths. Inhale for three counts, hold your breath for another three counts, then slowly exhale for three counts. Repeat this breathing pattern two more times.
4. Think about a situation that is troubling you at the moment. Replay the situation in your mind and bring up the thoughts and feelings that are usually triggered. Continue to focus on the situation, until the experience intensifies in your mind.
5. Pause and take a deep breath. Place a hand on your heart and ask yourself "What do you need right now?"
6. Recognize that the current emotional discomfort you are experiencing is rooted in past hurts. Be patient as you wait for your inner child to bring forth their unmet emotional needs.
7. You are welcome to reassure your inner child that it is safe to share their emotional needs. With your hand still on your heart, say "I promise to take your needs seriously because I desire to take care of you."

8. Continue to listen for a response. If you notice that your adult mind is trying to take over, shift your focus on your breathing for a few minutes, then back to listening for an answer.

9. If you are naturally a shy person, note that your inner child may exhibit the same trait too. It may take them a while to feel comfortable to share their needs with you. Reassure them that they don't need to share if they are not yet ready.

10. When your inner child does eventually share, acknowledge and write down what they tell you. Use their words, language, and phrasing, not your own. Tell them they are allowed to have these needs and you understand how they feel.

11. Before you end the meditation, ask them to provide suggestions on how you can respond to their needs. Once again, avoid switching to the adult mind and trying to rationalize these suggestions. Write down the spontaneous ideas you hear without self-correcting.

12. Thank your inner child for their courage and spend a moment thinking loving thoughts about them. Take three deep breaths and gently open your eyes.

Now that you have opened the lines of communication and practiced reaching out to your inner child, you are ready to move forward to the second stage of inner child healing—identifying past childhood wounds.

# REFLECTIONS

# STAGE 2
## Identify Past Childhood Wounds

# Do the Inner Child Work

Children don't have the cognitive skills or psychological tools to process trauma. As a result, they base their understanding of the world (and themselves) on the tragic experiences they have been through.

Inner child work seeks to uncover and heal childhood trauma once and for all. Now that you are an adult and can separate "who you are" from "what happened to you," it is possible to address emotional triggers, unmet needs, and other unwanted behavioral patterns that are trauma-informed.

The following exercises will help you begin inner child work. Note that you may feel vulnerable as you go through them, since they are designed to help you tap into a deeper part of yourself—perhaps a part of you that has been kept hidden for many years. But when you feel like holding back, remind yourself of the value of healing past wounds and granting your inner child the peace and closure they deserve.

## *Exercise 4: Wounded Inner Child Checklist*

What does a child do when they are unhappy? One child might throw a tantrum, another might withdraw from everybody, and another might turn to undesirable behaviors to get their parents' attention.

The same occurs when you have a wounded inner child. This traumatized aspect of you seeks out your attention through emotional outbursts, trauma-informed personality traits, and problematic behaviors. The aim is to get you to stop and address past wounds that continue to cause internal unrest.

Below is a checklist to discover the traits of a wounded inner child. The purpose isn't to make you feel judged or bad about yourself, but instead to show you what still needs to be healed inside of you.

Put an "X" next to each trait you display. Take your time and reflect on how you feel as you complete the checklist. Notice any themes or patterns that emerge and write them down for later review.

| Wounded Inner Child Traits | Tick "X" | Comments |
| --- | --- | --- |
| I think in black or white terms. E.g. People are either good or bad. | | |
| I consider myself a perfectionist. Aiming for the highest standards of achievement is normal. | | |
| I am often rigid and inflexible when things don't go the way I had planned. | | |
| I am fiercely independent and prefer to have control over every aspect of my life—including my relationships. | | |
| I am uncomfortable being playful and childlike. I take myself very seriously. | | |
| I have trouble feeling and expressing strong emotions or tolerating overly emotional people. | | |

| | | |
|---|---|---|
| I have trouble feeling and expressing strong emotions or tolerating overly emotional people. | | |
| I don't remember much about my early childhood years. | | |
| I tend to avoid emotional intimacy and feel uncomfortable about romantic commitment. | | |
| I avoid sharing personal thoughts or feelings because of being excessively distrustful of others. | | |
| I tend to avoid conflict and confrontations with others by either getting emotional, controlling the conversation, or withdrawing. | | |
| I am compulsive about or addicted to: drugs, alcohol, sex, work, competing, spending, fitness, or maintaining self-image. | | |
| I have family members or past romantic partners who were compulsive about or addicted to: drugs, alcohol, sex, work, competing, spending, fitness, or maintaining self-image. | | |

| I have a chronic feeling of emptiness, like something is missing in my life. | | |
| --- | --- | --- |

There are no scores for this checklist. The aim is for you to reflect on just how much trauma you may be carrying, which may need to be addressed through inner child work.

## *Exercise 5: Check Your Defenses*

One of the self-imposed barriers that can get in the way of your healing is defensiveness. Defensiveness is the tendency to shut down, deny, or deflect from perceived criticism. This makes it difficult to acknowledge the real issues and find ways to resolve them.

Indeed, bringing up the past is uncomfortable, and may threaten your sense of safety. However, the only way out is through, which means that past traumas and wounds must be confronted in order to be healed and released.

Here are a few reflection questions to check your defenses:

- Do you have a tendency to downplay or discount the impact of traumatic experiences in your childhood?

-------------------------------------------------------------------------------

-------------------------------------------------------------------------------

-------------------------------------------------------------------------------

- Do you have a tendency to normalize what was abnormal about past relationships?

-------------------------------------------------------------------------------

-------------------------------------------------------------------------------

-------------------------------------------------------------------------------

- Do you feel responsible to protect friends and family members who have hurt you in the past, out of fear of embarrassing them, compromising your relationships, or being ostracized?

-------------------------------------------------------------------------------

-------------------------------------------------------------------------------

-------------------------------------------------------------------------------

- Is there a part of you that believes you are permanently damaged and healing won't work?

-------------------------------------------------------------------------------

-------------------------------------------------------------------------------

-------------------------------------------------------------------------------

- Do you feel uncomfortable or react negatively when the past is brought up?

-------------------------------------------------------------------------------

-------------------------------------------------------------------------------

-------------------------------------------------------------------------------

Working through defensive behavior is the first step before undertaking inner child work. It is only when you are open to the process of healing and willing to let go of your defenses that old patterns, behaviors, and beliefs can be dismantled. The meditation below will help you begin to break through your defenses.

# Exercise 6: Meditation to Heal Defensiveness

Below is a meditation to expose and break through your defenses, so you can come close to the root of the pain.

Record yourself narrating the instructions below, then play the recording back to yourself.

Instructions for meditation:

1. Sit in a comfortable position on a chair.
2. Take a deep breath and when you exhale, allow the weight of your body to sink into the chair. Relax your face, neck, shoulders, and back.
3. Close your eyes and take deep breaths. Inhale for three counts, hold your breath for another three counts, then slowly exhale for three counts. Repeat this breathing pattern two more times.
4. Recall a painful childhood memory that you hardly think about. Travel back to that time in your mind and go through the details of what happened.
5. Pause the replay of the memory when you sense physical or mental resistance. Investigate which areas of your body feel tense, stiff, or sensitive. Rate the intensity of the resistance on a scale of 1–10 (10 being extremely intense).
6. Begin to heal the resistance by directing your breath to that tense body part. Inhale for three slow counts, hold your breath for three counts, then direct your "exhale" where you feel tension.
7. Continue this breathing pattern until the resistance feels less intense.

8. Return to the memory and pick up where you left off. The moment you feel resistance building up again, pause the replay and notice where the tension is coming from. Rate it out of 10 and heal the resistance by directing your breath to that area.

9. Each time you pause the memory, make a note of where you left off. Later on, this information can help you figure out which parts of the memory are most difficult to confront.

10. Please note that you don't have to replay the entire memory if it is still too painful to address. Congratulate yourself each time you are able to make small progress.

# *Exercise 7: Identify Emotional Triggers*

The benefit of being open about the past is that you get to understand where your emotional triggers come from, when they are activated, and how to avoid or reduce them.

Think about three to five different scenarios that trigger strong emotional reactions. These should be scenarios that elicit the same heightened emotions, nearly all of the time. For each scenario, answer the following questions:

- Describe the situation. What is happening? Where is it taking place? When does it usually happen? Who is often involved or present?

- What are your thoughts leading up to the trigger? What ideas or beliefs rush through your mind?

- What are your emotions leading up to the trigger? What physical sensations and feelings rush through your body?

-------------------------------------------------------------------

-------------------------------------------------------------------

-------------------------------------------------------------------

-------------------------------------------------------------------

-------------------------------------------------------------------

- What do you feel the urge to do? What is your usual reaction?

-------------------------------------------------------------------

-------------------------------------------------------------------

-------------------------------------------------------------------

-------------------------------------------------------------------

-------------------------------------------------------------------

- What event or memory from the past does this remind you of?

-------------------------------------------------------------------

-------------------------------------------------------------------

-------------------------------------------------------------------

-------------------------------------------------------------------

-------------------------------------------------------------------

-------------------------------------------------------------------

-------------------------------------------------------------------

-------------------------------------------------------------------

# Exercise 8: Revisiting Painful Memories

Communicating with your inner child can help you recognize and heal past childhood traumas and validate those troubling thoughts or painful emotions that still linger in your mind and body.

In a meditation session, similar to the ones you practiced in Stage 1, think about a painful childhood memory and ask your inner child how they felt when it happened, and how it impacted them. Listen carefully for their responses and write them down.

Alternatively, you can turn this into a reflection exercise and think about how your younger self handled a painful childhood event and the various ways it impacted you. Here are a few reflection questions to consider:

1. At the time, what did your younger self think was happening?
2. What events were taking place in your family at the time?
3. How did your younger self feel about what was happening?
4. Who did your younger self turn to? What type of support did they have?
5. What could others have done to help your younger self?
6. Did your younger self feel responsible to fix or control what was happening?
7. What coping behaviors did your younger self adopt to manage stress?
8. Are there any secrets your younger self kept to avoid causing further conflict?
9. What deep hurts are you still carrying from this painful childhood event?
10. If your younger self could tell you anything about that event, what would they say?

Identifying past childhood wounds is a difficult process. It requires you to relive painful memories that have been stored deep in your subconscious mind for many years. However, once you have completed this stage, you are ready to embrace your past, accept that you cannot change what happened, and begin to rewrite your life story. Let's proceed to stage 3 of inner child healing—practicing radical acceptance.

# REFLECTIONS

# STAGE 3
## Practice Radical Acceptance

# Accept What You Cannot Change

The Serenity Prayer is a short prayer recited in Alcohol Anonymous' 12-step program. It reminds people in recovery to accept their lives for what they are, not how they wish they could be. The prayer revolves around three powerful concepts: acceptance, change, and wisdom, and is recited like this (T, 2022):

*God, grant me the serenity*

*To accept the things I cannot change;*

*Courage to change the things I can;*

*and wisdom to know the difference.*

Radical acceptance is not the same as giving past traumas a stamp of approval. The tragic circumstances that happened to you or those you love cannot be erased from your mind or justified in any way. However, it is possible to accept that those events happened and you cannot go back and fix or change the outcomes.

Acceptance is the first step to healing, and later forgiveness. It is important to accept that life is not always good or pleasurable, and sometimes you are placed in situations that threaten your sense of safety. While you cannot control everything that happens to you, the decision to accept and move past those events rests with you.

The following exercises will help you practice radically accepting your life for what it is.

*Exercise 9: Meditation to Affirm Your Inner Child*

A wounded inner child may sometimes overreact or cause trouble for you because they desire your attention. Think of a child who is upset and can't seem to get the acknowledgment they desire from their parents.

When you sense fear, anxiety, insecurity, or loneliness, it may be a sign that your inner child requires emotional validation. All they want to know is that they are safe, loved, and accepted for who they are.

Below is a meditation to affirm your inner child and put them at ease. Record yourself narrating the instructions below, then play the recording back to yourself.

Instructions for meditation:

1. Sit in a comfortable position on a chair.
2. Take a deep breath and when you exhale, allow the weight of your body to sink into the chair. Relax your face, neck, shoulders, and back.
3. Close your eyes and take deep breaths. Inhale for three counts, hold your breath for another three counts, then slowly exhale for three counts. Repeat this breathing pattern two more times.
4. Think about a common challenge you experience at home, work, or within close relationships. For instance, you might have a habit of self-sabotaging, being a perfectionist, overworking, or not asking for help.
5. Focus on the emotions that are triggered each time you experience the challenge. For instance, do you feel stressed, out of control, or incompetent?

6. Validate those emotions by speaking directly to your inner child.
   Say a few words of affirmation to reassure them that they are safe,
   loved, capable, etc. For example, you might say to yourself:
     a. You are in safe hands.
     b. I am with you.
     c. I love you the way you are.
     d. I respect you.
     e. You mean everything to me.
     f. I am proud of you.
     g. It is okay to feel sad/anxious/misunderstood, etc.
7. Notice how your body feels after reciting a few affirmations.
   Remember to breathe through the discomfort.
8. After completing the meditation, identify one affirmation that
   struck a chord with you. Journal about your experience and why
   that particular affirmation made such a big impact.

# *Exercise 10: Fact-Check Your Beliefs*

Beliefs are shaped by the circumstances you experience and the outcome. Throughout your life, you have faced a number of adverse life situations that have birthed negative beliefs about yourself and others. But just because you think a certain way, doesn't make that thought true.

Think about negative beliefs that stem from adverse childhood experiences. These might include beliefs like:

*"I am dumb"*
*"I am not good enough"*
*"Nobody is trustworthy"*

As believable as they may have sounded to your younger self, they are not true. Go through the beliefs below and determine which column they fall under in your personal life: fact or opinion. Give evidence to justify your choice.

| Belief | Fact | Opinion | Evidence |
|---|---|---|---|
| I am a reject. | | | |
| I am unlovable. | | | |
| My job is stressful. | | | |
| The world is evil. | | | |

| | | | |
|---|---|---|---|
| **Nobody likes me.** | | | |
| **People will always disappoint you.** | | | |
| **I am overweight.** | | | |
| **I am not good enough.** | | | |
| **My family is judgmental** | | | |
| **I am unattractive.** | | | |
| **I am not happy about the quality of my friendships.** | | | |

## *Exercise 11: Tap Into Logical Mind*

Your logical mind is the part of you that looks for factual evidence to justify experiences. Whenever you are feeling upset, it is important to first take a moment to calm down, then ask objective questions about what is happening and how you might be possibly affected.

Think of a recent situation that made you emotional. Answer the following objective questions to practice thinking with your logical mind:

- Provide facts about what happened. Mention what you could see, hear, touch/feel, taste, or smell.

------------------------------------------------------------

------------------------------------------------------------

------------------------------------------------------------

------------------------------------------------------------

------------------------------------------------------------

- What recent events led to this situation?

------------------------------------------------------------

------------------------------------------------------------

------------------------------------------------------------

------------------------------------------------------------

------------------------------------------------------------

- What was your role in the unfolding of this situation? Think about what you said, the actions you took, or the position you played.

------------------------------------------------------------

------------------------------------------------------------

------------------------------------------------------------

- Which aspects of this situation do you have the power to change? Write down three suggestions of possible changes within your control.

--------------------------------------------------------------------

--------------------------------------------------------------------

--------------------------------------------------------------------

--------------------------------------------------------------------

--------------------------------------------------------------------

- Which aspects of this situation do you NOT have the power to change? Write down three real constraints that you cannot control.

--------------------------------------------------------------------

--------------------------------------------------------------------

--------------------------------------------------------------------

--------------------------------------------------------------------

--------------------------------------------------------------------

- How did you react during and after the situation? And what impact did your reaction have on others?

--------------------------------------------------------------------

--------------------------------------------------------------------

--------------------------------------------------------------------

--------------------------------------------------------------------

--------------------------------------------------------------------

- Could you have reacted differently? If so, how?

# *Exercise 12: Embrace Reality*

Embracing reality is about focusing on what is happening right now. For instance, you may still be upset with an ex about how they treat you, but the reality is that you are no longer in that relationship and those strong feelings shouldn't hold you back from meeting someone incredible.

The trick to embracing reality is to adjust your thinking so that it is neither too negative or too positive. Ideally, your thoughts should be fair (i.e. trusting that your life outcomes can change at any moment) and balanced.

Go through the following list of negative statements and turn them into fair and balanced statements.

| Negative Statement | Fair and Balanced Statement |
| --- | --- |
| E.g. I am a failure. | I have failed in the past and let myself down, but I am not defined by my low moments. |
| My parents ruined my life. | |
| I will never heal from my past trauma. | |
| I attract toxic people into my life. | |
| My situation will never change. | |
| Psychotherapy doesn't work for me. | |
| I am a lost cause. | |

| | |
|---|---|
| **If people knew my life story, they wouldn't accept me.** | |
| **I am not smart enough to go to college.** | |
| **I am a disappointment to my life.** | |
| **Most people don't like me.** | |
| **I will be single for the rest of my life.** | |
| **I can never forgive certain people for what they have done.** | |
| **There is no point in living this life.** | |

Radical acceptance is saying, "My life isn't perfect, but it is still my life." Your life story has many highs and lows, but you are not defined by either of them. Embrace each season of your life, whether pleasant or unpleasant, and instead of resisting the not-so-pleasant, ask yourself, "What valuable life lessons can I learn from this experience?"

The following stage after radically accepting your life is to refocus on the inner child and reparent yourself.

# REFLECTIONS

# STAGE 4
## Reparent yourself

# Be the Parent You Never Had

They say a child's first love and first heartbreak is experienced with their parents. In many ways, this is true.

None can deny the importance of that parent-child bond in forming healthy attachments, building a sense of self, and learning to believe in yourself. When this bond starts to feel unsafe and unreliable, other relationships feel threatening, and you may even doubt your own self-worth.

If you were raised by unconscious parents, who were perhaps emotionally neglectful, controlling, alcoholics, or suffered from mental illness, you may have missed out on the security, nurturing, and guidance you needed to develop a healthy sense of self and feel confident navigating through life.

Part of inner child healing is being the parent you never had by responding to those unmet emotional needs and validating that lonely, scared, or abandoned inner child. It is about showing up for yourself, rather than waiting on others to show up for you. No one else knows what you need or desire better than you, therefore you are the best substitute parent to take over where your parents left off.

The following exercises will present different ways to reparent yourself.

## *Exercise 13: What Parent Do You Want to Be?*

As you begin your reparenting journey, decide on what kind of parent you want to be. In other words, how do you intend on relating with yourself and responding to your needs?

On the line space provided below, brainstorm the type of characteristics you wish to adopt that are qualities of a conscious and loving parent. Next to each characteristic, write down ways that you can practice showing up in that manner.

For example, if you desire to be open and nonjudgmental, you can practice journaling about your experiences and validating your thoughts and feelings.

Here is a short list of qualities of a conscious and loving parent:
- Empathetic
- Nurturing
- Understanding
- Dedicated
- Supportive
- Disciplined
- Faithful
- Organized
- Patient
- Good listener

## Exercise 14: Make a Promise

It is important for your inner child to trust that you can respond to their needs. Make a small promise to yourself everyday that you can confidently keep. For instance, you might promise to:

- Check-in with yourself during the day.
- Eat a healthy breakfast.
- Recite a positive affirmation.
- Journal before going to bed.

Make sure that you fulfill whatever goal or task you have set, and at the end of the week, reflect on the promises you kept and how they are helping you improve your quality of life.

# *Exercise 15: What Do You Need Right Now?*

Set an alarm to ring once a day, when you are able to take a five-minute break. The purpose of the break is to ask yourself a simple question, "What do I need right now?" and respond with whatever prompting you intuitively feel.

When asking this question, tune into what you are sensing in your body. You might pick up on various needs, such as:

- Physical needs (e.g. food, water, warmth, silence, fresh air, hug, etc.).
- Psychological needs (e.g. validation, respect, affection, positive energy, peace, etc.).
- Social needs (e.g. intimacy, support, adventure, sense of belonging, uplifting conversation, etc.).

Focus on addressing a need with an activity that can be performed within the allotted time (five minutes). For example, if you need positive energy, call a friend or watch funny memes online.

## *Exercise 16: Meditation to Explore Your Own Love Languages*

An insecure attachment between a parent and a child is created when a parent ignores or neglects their child's physical, mental, and emotional needs. In other words, they are unable to communicate and respond to their child's love language. Reparenting yourself presents an opportunity to explore your inner child's love language (or several love languages), and connect to their deeper needs.

Before you begin the meditation, familiarize yourself with the five love languages, as described by Gary Chapman in his book, The 5 Love Languages (Chapman, 2015). Below are examples of how you would respond to each of your love languages:

- Words of affirmation: Using positive self-talk to feel loved and supported.
- Acts of service: Engaging in self-care practices to express love and gratitude.
- Receiving gifts: Buying yourself small, thoughtful gifts to feel loved.
- Quality time: Spending alone time with yourself to recharge and quiet your mind.
- Physical touch: Embracing your body and comforting yourself through intentional touch.

The meditation below encourages you to explore your inner child's love languages. Record yourself narrating the instructions below, then play the recording back to yourself.

Instructions for meditation:

1. Sit in a comfortable position on a chair.

2. Take a deep breath and when you exhale, allow the weight of your body to sink into the chair. Relax your face, neck, shoulders, and back.

3. Close your eyes and take deep breaths. Inhale for three counts, hold your breath for another three counts, then slowly exhale for three counts. Repeat this breathing pattern two more times.

4. Think back to three childhood experiences that made you feel adored. Start with the first one and recall where you were, who you were with, and what was happening. Connect to the thoughts, emotions, or actions that made you feel loved. What exactly was it?

5. Consider which of the five love languages was being represented at that moment, and how exactly it was being expressed. For example, if the love language was words of affirmation, think about or write down the exact words that were spoken to you; or if you were given a gift, note what gift it was and why it felt significant.

6. When you are ready, move on to the second childhood experience and repeat steps 4 and 5. Notice whether the love language represented is the same, or different. Finally, reflect on the third childhood experience and repeat the steps. Notice if any new love language comes up, or whether the same one keeps on emerging.

7. Take three deep breaths and end the meditation. Spend another 10 minutes researching the love languages that were identified, and practical ways that you can respond to them.

## *Exercise 17: Fill the Gaps*

There were certain cognitive, social, and emotional skills that you were unable to learn as a child due to them not being taught or reinforced at home. These might include skills like how to set boundaries, self-monitoring, managing strong emotions, or being an assertive communicator.

On the line space provided below, make a list of the skills you never learned as a child. Examples of important childhood skills are:

- Maintaining focus
- Self-control
- Assertive communication
- Setting healthy boundaries
- Critical thinking
- Problem-solving
- Emotional intelligence
- Healthy risk-taking
- Making social connections

For each skill, create a SMART goal that you can work on for a specific length of time. SMART stands for specific, measurable, achievable, relevant, and time-bound. Goals that are structured using this technique help you set clear objectives that are realistic.

For example, if you desire to teach yourself self-control, you might create a SMART goal related to monitoring your social media usage. Using the basic structure, your goal might be defined as follows: To spend a maximum of 20 minutes per day browsing through social media platforms, for a period of two weeks. Keep the first few goals small enough to successfully complete. Once you have built a habit, try setting more challenging goals, or exploring different skills.

The final stage of inner child healing is rebuilding your life as you envision and creating your new normal.

# REFLECTIONS

# STAGE 5
## Create New Norms

# Rebuild Your Life

The aim of inner child healing is to help you get closure from the past, so you can focus on creating the life of your dreams. Rebuilding your life starts by making a u-turn, and choosing to go the opposite direction of where your trauma was taking you. For instance, instead of going the route of low self-esteem, toxic relationships, and self-destructive behaviors, you choose to go the route of self-awareness, healthy habits, and personal growth.

It is important for you to believe that you actually can heal from past trauma and unlearn harmful behavioral patterns. Say this to yourself each morning: "I have it in me to heal and outgrow old patterns," then visualize yourself transforming into a better version of yourself.

The following exercises will help you begin the process of rebuilding your life and practicing seeing yourself and your life differently.

## *Exercise 18: Gratitude Letter to Yourself*

Write a letter to yourself and reflect on goals you have accomplished or challenges you have overcome over the years. Highlight the personal strengths or positive qualities that stood out for you, and what you have learned about yourself from those experiences. The tone of the letter should remain positive and motivational. The letter should also focus on you, not other people.

Below are a few lines to write your gratitude letter:

# *Exercise 19: Come Out of Your Comfort Zone*

If you have ever suffered from post-traumatic stress disorder (or may still be in the process of healing from it), you will know how difficult it can be to embrace change. Your habits and routines are what helped you rebuild a sense of safety after being destabilized by past painful events, so venturing out into the unknown and exploring new experiences seems frightening.

However, there is no growth that occurs inside your comfort zone. For as long as you stay there, you will continue to go through the same cycles, repeat the same patterns, and feel dissatisfied with your life. There are no guarantees that you won't fail when you try something new, but one thing is for certain—you will grow!

Below are some journal prompts to help you get comfortable with the idea of getting out of your comfort zone:

- How does the "unknown" or "uncertainty" make you feel?

--------------------------------------------------------------------

--------------------------------------------------------------------

--------------------------------------------------------------------

- On a scale of 1–10 (10 being very satisfied), how satisfied are you with your life right now?

--------------------------------------------------------------------

--------------------------------------------------------------------

--------------------------------------------------------------------

- What do you know with absolute certainty needs to change?

--------------------------------------------------------------------

--------------------------------------------------------------------

--------------------------------------------------------------------

- What are the advantages of being in your comfort zone?

------------------------------------------------------------

------------------------------------------------------------

------------------------------------------------------------

- What are the risks of remaining in your comfort zone?

------------------------------------------------------------

------------------------------------------------------------

------------------------------------------------------------

- What are you afraid might happen if you chase after your dreams?

------------------------------------------------------------

------------------------------------------------------------

------------------------------------------------------------

- Write a list of tasks or behaviors that are outside of your comfort zone and muster the courage to practice one each week or month.

------------------------------------------------------------

------------------------------------------------------------

------------------------------------------------------------

------------------------------------------------------------

------------------------------------------------------------

------------------------------------------------------------

------------------------------------------------------------

- Think about a short-term goal and write down a rough plan of how you would achieve it.

- Describe your ideal morning, work day, or weekend, and reflect on how you can make it a reality.

- Write down your daily routine. Find tasks that you can tweak or do differently.

# Exercise 20: Create a Movie of Your Life

Lay down on your bed, facing the ceiling, and close your eyes. Imagine that you are watching a movie about a typical day in your life. Notice the details, such as where you live, who you are with, what you are doing, and how you feel. Play the movie in slow motion and savor each moment. Connect to the experience as though it were happening in real life. Set aside time each day to replay the movie of your life.

## *Exercise 21: Celebrate Daily Wins*

Get into the habit of noticing positive actions that you are taking to rebuild your life. Each day, catch yourself doing something positive, productive, healthy, or generous, and write it down. By the end of the day, you should have a list of daily wins that you can celebrate. How you decide to celebrate is completely up to you! It could be as simple as scheduling 30 minutes of alone time or taking a relaxing bubble bath.

## *Exercise 22: Increase Spiritual Awareness*

Spirituality is the process of getting to a deeper part of you. This "deeper part of you" could be your Higher Power, subconscious mind, mother nature, or any other energy or entity. Spiritual practices are the gateways to access that deeper part of you and heighten your sense of awareness.

Create a list of spiritual practices that you practice, or are curious about. Your list may include practices like:

- Meditation
- Walking in nature
- Prayer
- Yoga
- Journaling
- Hypnotherapy
- Listening to nature sounds
- Reading religious texts

For each practice, answer the following question:

- What is your understanding of this practice? What is its purpose? How can it help you?

------------------------------------------------------------

------------------------------------------------------------

------------------------------------------------------------

------------------------------------------------------------

------------------------------------------------------------

- What steps are involved in this practice? What are the requirements?

------------------------------------------------------------

------------------------------------------------------------

------------------------------------------------------------

------------------------------------------------------------

------------------------------------------------------------

- What reviews have you heard about this practice? How has it helped other people?

------------------------------------------------------------

------------------------------------------------------------

------------------------------------------------------------

------------------------------------------------------------

------------------------------------------------------------

- How might you incorporate this practice into your daily routine?
  How many minutes can you dedicate? Which time of day would
  be most suitable?

-------------------------------------------------------------------

-------------------------------------------------------------------

-------------------------------------------------------------------

-------------------------------------------------------------------

-------------------------------------------------------------------

-------------------------------------------------------------------

- What obstacles might get in the way of you doing this practice
  regularly? How can you prevent these obstacles?

-------------------------------------------------------------------

-------------------------------------------------------------------

-------------------------------------------------------------------

-------------------------------------------------------------------

-------------------------------------------------------------------

-------------------------------------------------------------------

## *Exercise 23: Personal Growth Quiz*

Trauma doesn't have to be how your life story ends. It can be the catalyst for positive change. The "old you" that existed before going through the suffering is gone. However, in that person's place is the "new you" who has a deeper appreciation for life and others.

The following quiz will help you assess the progress you are making, based on the key components of personal growth:

- Appreciation for life.
- Deepening spirituality.
- Improving relationships with others.
- Discovering personal strengths.
- Learning new perspectives.
- Tapping into your creativity.

Reflect on where you are currently in your life and rate each statement below on a scale of 1–7 (1 = not important, 7 = very important).

| Statements | Ratings (1-7) |
|---|---|
| 1. I have discovered interest. | |
| 2. I am more optimistic than before. | |
| 3. I am actively changing what needs to be changed. | |
| 4. My priorities have shifted. | |

| | |
|---|---|
| 5. I love my life. | |
| 6. I am open to closeness and intimacy with people. | |
| 7. I am more spiritual than before. | |
| 8. I feel empathetic towards others. | |
| 9. I recognize new opportunities. | |
| 10. I feel strong. | |
| 11. I live a purpose-driven life. | |
| 12. I am creative. | |
| 13. I lean on my support system. | |
| 14. I have discovered my passions. | |
| 15. I have redefined my values. | |
| 16. I am aware of my own worth. | |
| 17. I believe there are good people in the world. | |
| 18. I am more playful than before. | |

| | |
|---|---|
| 19. People have noticed a positive change in me. | |
| 20. I know what is within and outside of my control. | |
| 21. I have more faith than before. | |
| 22. I enjoy asking questions and solving problems. | |
| 23. I have a light-hearted approach to life. | |
| 24. I care about humans, animals, and the planet. | |
| 25. I frequently practice visualization. | |
| 26. I am aware that I have options in life. | |
| 27. I invest more time and energy into relationships. | |
| 28. I desire more meaning in life. | |
| 29. I am aware of my potential. | |
| 30. I have learned how to set and achieve goals. | |

Add up the totals for each category using the following guideline:

| Personal Growth Category | Questions | Total Points by Category |
|---|---|---|
| Appreciation for life | 2; 4; 15; 20; 23 | |
| Deepening spiritiality | 7; 11; 21; 24; 28 | |
| Improving relationships with others | 6; 8; 13; 17; 27 | |
| Discovering personal strengths | 5; 10; 14, 16; 19 | |
| Learning new perspectives | 1; 3; 9; 26; 29 | |
| Tapping into your creativity | 12; 18; 22; 25; 30 | |

Based on the quiz, which areas of personal growth are you making the most and least progress? Take this quiz every quarter (once in three months) to reevaluate your personal growth.

# REFLECTIONS

# AFFIRMATIONS

# Affirmations

Affirmations are short, powerful sentences that you could repeat to yourself. When we get older, we tend to stop listening to our inner child's needs. Also, our experiences throughout life made us believe some assumptions about ourselves. Sometimes these assumptions are very strong but not true. They will stand in the way of our adult selves and our inner child.

It is important to have positive assumptions about yourself and your abilities.

In the following list, you find some inspiration for positive affirmations related to the inner child. Pick a few that resonated with you and try to say them out loud at least one time a day. Try to really feel something when you say them not just say them out loud.

- I am confident in myself and the things I can accomplish
- I can follow my childhood dreams
- I am strong
- I am loveable
- I am capable of everything I set my mind to
- I accept my inner child and allow it back into my life
- I am filled with positive energy
- I allow myself to be vulnerable and authentic, just like a little child
- I am free to be the person I always dreamed of being
- I can express myself in a safe space
- I can learn everything that I am open to
- I am surrounded by light and love
- I am at peace with myself
- I am grateful for the lessons that I have encountered in my life
- I am able to make beautiful things
- I am beautiful in every single way
- I give myself the freedom of fun and playfulness

- I release everything I do not need anymore
- I can nurture my inner child
- I can grow
- I deserve to heal myself
- I choose to help my inner child
- I love myself unconditionally
- I am growing into the best version of me
- I am enough
- I can achieve greatness
- I see my confidence grow everyday
- I love myself unconditionally
- I am safe
- I can let go everything that is not serving me anymore
- I am protected
- I am worthy of love
- I am free to choose the life I want
- I can achieve anything my inner child had in mind
- I am worthy of love
- I choose to believe in myself
- I am on my way to becoming the best version of myself
- I trust my intuition and inner guidance
- I can support my inner child
- I celebrate my inner child
- I am open to learn and grow
- I embrace all part of myself
- I am a powerful being
- I am in control
- I am trying and learning everyday
- I am grateful I am here
- I express myself freely
- I am in charge of my own decisions, emotions, and life
- I choose happiness and health
- I am healing

# REFLECTIONS

# CONCLUSION

I'VE PROMISED MY INNER CHILD THAT NEVER AGAIN WILL I EVER
ABANDON MYSELF FOR ANYTHING OR ANYONE ELSE AGAIN.
-RWYNONNA JUDD

Inner child healing is the journey of reconciling the past with the present so that you are no longer haunted by what happened. This journey isn't an easy one, since it requires confronting childhood trauma, making sense of what happened, and choosing to accept it for what it is.

Your wounded inner child will continue to seek your attention until you have made peace with the past and received the closure you deserve. Sometimes this may be through emotional outbursts, limiting beliefs, or self-destructive behaviors. Instead of pretending that nothing is wrong and that you don't sense the inner emptiness, you can pay attention to your inner child and help them heal from past hurts.

The exercises offered in this workbook have been compiled to help you get through the five stages of inner child healing, which include:

***Stage 1: Reach Out to Your Inner Child***

***Stage 2: Identify Past Childhood Wounds***

***Stage 3: Practice Radical Acceptance***

***Stage 4: Reparent Yourself***

***Stage 5: Create New Norms***

Nevertheless, the responsibility to do the internal work and maintain a connection with your inner child rests with you. It is important to recognize that at any point, you can rewrite the story of your life, reframe your beliefs, and adopt behaviors that promote a healthy and healed self. All this power lies within you!

I hope that by going through these exercises and prompts, you have been encouraged to look at yourself and your life differently and continue pressing forward on your healing journey. Pain, loss, and misfortune are inevitable life experiences—and inner child healing won't make you immune to them. However, with greater self-awareness, you can learn to embrace the highs and lows, victories and losses, and see them as being a part of the greater work of finding yourself and living a meaningful life.

Nothing happens by accident. The good and bad circumstances of the past have led you to where you are right now. You are exactly where you are supposed to be, doing what you are meant to be doing. Look ahead and see the possibilities of what your life might look like. The only way is forward!

# REFLECTIONS

# BONUS: Your Free Gift

I'm only offering this bonus for FREE to my readers. This is a way of saying thank you for your purchase. In this gift, you will find a guide with extra tools to start your inner journey.

### *Healing Your Inner Child First Guide*

*Embark on a Transformative Inner Journey to Rediscover Your Inner Child with Extraordinary Tools!*

### *Inside this book, you'll discover:*
- How to use journaling in the healing process.
- Questions to remember your Inner Child.
- Space to write your thoughts down.
- Questions to better understand your Inner Child's pain.
- Motivational things to say to your Inner Child.
- Positive affirmations + 5-step method to make your own.
- An extra Inner Child meditation.
- A checklist.
- And more...

# Thank You

I really appreciate you for purchasing my book!

You had the chance to pick many other books, but you chose this one.

So, **thank you so much** for purchasing this book and reading it to the very last page! I hope that I was able to help you in your healing process, as my goal is to help as many people as possible!

Before you close the book, I want to ask for **a small favor**. Would you please consider *leaving an honest review* about the book? **This would be really helpful for me**, as I'm an independent author and posting reviews is the best and easiest way to support me.

The review you provide will help me so I can continue selling, improving, and writing books. **It will mean the world to me to hear from you.**

Go to this book and scroll down (https://mybook.to/inner-child-workbook), or scan the QR code to leave a review:

<table>
<tr><td>Amazon US</td><td>Amazon UK</td><td>Rest of the World</td></tr>
</table>

# References

Chapman, G. D. (2015). The 5 love languages. Northfield Pub. (Original work published 1992)

Compitus, K. (2020, October 20). 12 Radical acceptance worksheets for your DBT sessions. PositivePsychology.com. https://positivepsychology.com/radical-acceptance-worksheets/#worksheets

Dutta, M. (2022, December 30). Top 80 inner child quotes to help you heal. Kidadl.com. https://kidadl.com/quotes/top-inner-child-quotes-to-help-you-hea

Gerlach, P. K. (2015, March 30). Checklist: Common behavioral traits of psychological wounds. http://sfhelp.org/gwc/1_traits.htm

Goal Chaser. (2021, September 20). Radical acceptance quotes for healing. The Goal Chaser. https://thegoalchaser.com/radical-acceptance-quotes/

Ludlam, J. (2020, January 8). Celebrate new beginnings with these inspirational quotes. Country Living. https://www.countryliving.com/life/g30337217/new-beginnings-quotes/

T, B. (2022, March 4). How is the serenity prayer used in 12-step groups? Verywell Mind. https://www.verywellmind.com/the-serenity-prayer-62614#:~:text=The%20Serenity%20Prayer%20reminds%20people

www.ingramcontent.com/pod-product-compliance
Lightning Source LLC
LaVergne TN
LVHW041226200726
843507LV00013B/2599